HOW THE SKY GOT ITS STARS

A HOPI LEGEND

RETOLD BY GAIL TUCHMAN

COLLAGES BY SUSAN L. ROTH

HARCOURT BRACE & COMPANY

Orlando   Atlanta   Austin   Boston   San Francisco   Chicago   Dallas   New York
Toronto   London

Long ago, when the Earth was new, all of the animals helped make things.

All but Coyote.

The animals made lakes,
but Coyote just watched.
The animals made hills,
but Coyote just watched.

The animals made trees,
but Coyote just watched.

One day the animals made lots and lots of small, bright things.

"What can we do with them?"
they asked.

"Maybe we could put them in the lakes," said one.
"Maybe we could put them on the hills," said another.

"Maybe we could hang them in the trees," said another. They could not decide.

So they went to sleep.

While they slept, Coyote looked around. He picked up one of the small, bright things. "I can't play with this," he said. So he threw it far up into the air.

Coyote picked up another. "I can't eat this," he said. So he threw it far up into the air.

Coyote picked up each one of the small, bright things. "I can't use these," he said. So he threw them all far up into the air.

Then Coyote looked up at the night sky, and saw all of the small, bright things shining in the dark.

And that is how Coyote helped put the stars in the sky.